Informant vs Inmate

The Covert War Against The Black Vote

By

Melvin Prince Johnakin

Informant vs Inmate

The Covert War Against The Black Vote

Copyright 2022 by Melvin Prince Johnakin

All rights reserved. No part of this publication may be reproduced, distributed, or transmitted in any form or by any means, including photocopying, recording, or other electronic or mechanical methods, without the prior written permission of the publisher, except in the case of brief quotations embodied in critical reviews and certain other noncommercial uses permitted by copyright law.

Although the author and publisher have made every effort to ensure that the information in this book was correct at press time, the author and publisher do not assume and hereby disclaim any liability to any party for any loss, damage, or disruption caused by errors or omissions, whether such errors or omissions result from negligence, accident, or any other cause.

Adherence to all applicable laws and regulations, including international, federal, state and local governing professional licensing, business practices, advertising, and all other aspects of doing business in the US, Canada or any other jurisdiction is the sole responsibility of the reader and consumer.

Neither the author nor the publisher assumes any responsibility or liability whatsoever on behalf of the consumer or reader of this material. Any perceived slight of any individual or organization is purely unintentional.

The resources in this book are provided for informational purposes only and should not be used to replace the specialized training and professional judgment of a health care or mental health care professional.

Neither the author nor the publisher can be held responsible for the use of the information provided within this book. Please always consult a trained professional before making any decision regarding treatment of yourself or others.

Dedication

To my **INTEGRITY HERO:**

I have found that ***Kelvin Jeremiah*** has not just focused on housing for low-income residents of Philadelphia, but he has also focused on the dualism of literacy and education as an individual possession and communally embedded commodity. He asserted that access to literacy is achieved through schools, but access to education may be accomplished only through mutual understanding, respect for the community, and a sense of cultural identity.

Kelvin Jeremiah (born December 15, 1972, Grenada) is President and C.E.O. of the Philadelphia Housing Authority. Jeremiah accepted a position at the Philadelphia Housing Authority (PHA) in August 2011. He became the agency's first Director of Audit and Compliance, in which he instituted policies designed to ferret out WASTE, FRAUD, ABUSE and MISMANAGEMENT.

Jeremiah became the Housing Urban and Development (HUD) - appointed Administration Receiver and them Interim Executive Director of PHA. He was appointed President and C.E.O. of PHA in March 2013, and within his first month, they were able to return to local control.

GREAT JOB!

Forward

There is no generally accepted definition of *" White - Collar Crime. "* For the purposes of this book, it will be defined as crimes committed by persons in government, the professions and business in their occupational roles.

It includes: embezzlement, antitrust - law violations, business swindles, corruption of public officials, income tax evasion, stock frauds, defrauding the government food and drug law violations, consumer frauds and management and Union collusion. Many *" White -Collar Criminals "* are persons of high status and social standing whose offenses are committed in the course of their respective work.

We can define the problem in these terms: after 350 years of constant tendon attendant upon efforts to absorb the Black into American democracy, there are now new areas of difficulty because the Black minority has decided to push for its rights rather than permit matters to move at their own pace.

Some might think aspects of the problem are the belated granting of Black legal equality. But both Black and White Americans have learned the hard way that legal equality is a necessary precondition to, but not a sufficient condition for, the effective absorption of the Black into American life.

Dr. Melvin Prince Johnakin

Table of Contents

Introduction 5

Chapter 1 - Representation 8

Chapter 2 - Partners in Crime 12

Chapter 3 - Good Intentions Twisted 19

Chapter 4 - The Lights Dimmed 27

Chapter 5 - When The Elite Top 50 Isn't Enough 33

Chapter 6 - The Inevitable 42

Chapter 7 - When Change Has A New Face 48

Chapter 8 - Dark Doors 56

Chapter 9 - The Lit Match to Democracy 64

Introduction

I get it, some will take offense to this book simply based on Race, which is the very reason I wrote it to underline the grave injustice some blacks are committed to uphold unknowingly, despite the economic and cultural war against your family, and community by those to whom you pledge allegiance.

Here's a glimpse of the murky dichotomy that many blacks haven't fully embraced as a real operation against their well-being, but its inner workings have diminished, and even eliminated substantial progress for decades on large scales. Many persuasions ask, "Why do blacks predominately vote for Black Democratic candidates? I mean, we understand historically the need for the United States to open its political corridors for inclusion, but not principally because a person is of a particular race." Their assessment was duly noted. Just look at the flop before us that President Biden forced Blacks to accept… There is NO representation for black people. VP Kamala Harris has absolutely zero commitment to the Black community so, are we to settle for this attractive Caribbean Southeast Asian as the sum blacks fought decades to see? Though Joe thinks we should throw our support, I think not. She, along with other Democrats, like Barack Obama had no problems in telling the world, "I don't represent black people only". Though this is correct, but could we at least get some representation for something that benefits blacks and doesn't equate to a water-down handout? Can we for once get some real business on the table, i.e.., procurement – contracts – where the real business that Whites have benefited from since its inception. Trust me, we have qualified people; they just need an open door that the system has maintained to keep closed with a tight grip and is extremely selective about who enters this world.

It must be said Black Americans should get comfortable being uncomfortable in addressing the age-old question; do we need a political Savior? Unequivocally it is personally gratifying to see representation of the same hue, but this cannot be the primary criteria. What many devoted blacks haven't settled within themselves is the degree of misrepresentation that takes place where blacks are sold and pillaged as a commodity to the highest bidder. Not just by Black politicians but also the clergy. Everybody gets to have access to us for the least.

The little secret that impacts Blacks on colossal scales is not understanding who is representing us: Informants or Inmates. And if either of these personalities have been issued a "Target Letter", which I'll get more into later, but this is a serious area of concern and is one the most effective Jim Crow methods that have blocked, canceled out, and continues to eliminate success for millions of Black people, and they don't even know how.

It's very late in the political game; laws are still passing in many states to block Black ascension, but Black people must pull up, take responsibility and ownership of your future. As a "People" we can no longer be okay with chintzy campaign promises that end up as fragmented programs with the dish-out of a few dollars to create the appearance of caring about you and respect for your vote. The measurements are always short-term. What gives?

As we review the historical contributions of blacks in America and the intense struggle to have fair play; open access to trade, politics, academia and global participation, there is no way African Americans can continue to see "Color" when voting while the big picture is "global participation", and we aren't even invited to the table.

Blacks could be so much further along economically if they had aligned themselves with Trump's philosophy: "What do you have to lose?" To at least rethink their vote and who is representing them in D.C. and in state and local races in lieu of casting a vote just because of familiarity.

Many Black business owners understand this wholeheartedly – we will continue to lose when we fail to hold any of the elected officials, we put into office who do not fight to represent the interest and well-being of our community. And for this reason, Blacks cannot continue to arbitrarily vote for Black candidates or Democratic.

We need to push pause and look at what others are empowered to do economically versus what Black businesses have access to; there is NO comparison. How long will we settle for crumbs from the table when the spread is before us?

What the PAST should have taught us: Nothing from nothing leaves nothing. There is little to no representation legislatively for Black people. Only we can change the scorecard.

Chapter 1

Representation

One of the biggest political *misnomers* enshrined in the consciousness of some blacks who selectively cast their votes based on culture, gender, and Race is that having a Black in office would guarantee an ally. Some believe their loyalty will be rewarded with a champion to fight against injustice and specifically take up their cultural causes.

The voting bloc, though diverse in education, economics, and cultural enrichment, sometimes prevent themselves from expanding their knowledge base or elect different types of candidates because of generational influences. At the dinner table, conversations with Big Mama are about how everyone needs to vote for Democrats so that community programs will continue, or housing vouchers are extended. Sadly, the young female in the residence sees a model that says, "It's okay to have a baby without resources because we'll depend on external support." These conversations are often in the earshot of the youngest, most impressionable children in the household who are being molded to think about scarcity and do not know it. A new generation is indoctrinated just to get by.

Low-information voters very seldom research a candidate's agenda or what they have supported in the past, and even if they never held an office but worked with opposing parties that marginalize Blacks economically, this should be a big concern. In addition, certainly they should not be given the honor of being elected.

As a "group," Blacks cannot afford to continue with a nondescript, haphazard approach to the economic war that's waged against them and upheld by crooked Black politicians fronting and faking with enticing campaign speeches. They have absolutely no intention of sponsoring or co-sponsoring legislation that could create a path to educate poverty-stricken youth or fight for access to business capital for Black businesses that would guarantee opportunity.

The allegiance of Black voters to the Democratic Party is as a narrative that reads like a horror story; we already know the setup, and who dies first. At some point, we have to stop being the ones forced to keep taking one for the team and always on defense because we are sold out at every level. We have to equip ourselves with the power of information and learn the process of how to move forward with partners who will work with us.

There are serious questions to ask and cultural positions that need to change if we are to pull ourselves from the mire of misrepresentation and sellouts. If Blacks do not learn to expect better and demand more when confronted with bias opportunities, nothing will ever change.

The smooth-talking, well-dressed speechmaker often is let off the hook without any accountability to the people because he or she seems friendly and cool. Some of their involvements in efforts to connect with everyday people are misplaced priorities and marginalized, though there is merit to creating connectivity with the least of them. Notwithstanding, blacks must learn to exercise more of their critical thinking skills when politicians show up with trinkets to keep voters tethered.

Black politicians often use politically sponsored community picnics or cookouts as the smallest means to show appreciation for their poor voting group. This is misleading and a method to just hang out and stay visible, instead of having substantive town halls to hear what the community really needs. Stop making a big deal about the little things... Nor should the seasonal turkey giveaways during Thanksgiving and Christmas, or the back-to-school jamboree with the moon bounce and water ice be considered monumental when other people are getting access to Capital. These jesters are nice but are some of the lowest forms used to say, "Thank You."

This cannot be the highest return for black support. The black vote is worth billions, and if blacks are going to build generational wealth, somebody has to raise the stakes and push for "procurement opportunities."

However, if we as a people continue to settle for ineffective lawmakers, the marginalization we have experienced is nobody's fault but ours. The political system is still killing dreams and cascading hopes for a better future down the drain because measurable success comes about when the right partners are in concert. Moreover, Blacks have fallen repeatedly for the dance with the devil, and each time the outcomes are being more fragmented and worth less in value.

Black voters have to open their eyes, and when they realize, nobody is coming to save them on a white horse and reshape their landscape to give them a competitive edge economically, the voting block will shift.

The complicity to uphold candidates based on race and gender is undoing 100 years of struggle for Blacks in

America. Somebody please take the rose-colored glasses off. It is about representation and access.

Chapter 2

Partners in Crime

What if your favorite television crime series mirrors a direct link to the criminal element in law enforcement and politics in your backyard? From staging, evading justice, illegal corporate and community shakedowns, business, and personal oppression, and how some successfully continue their criminal empire under the camouflage of public service. Amazing is it not?

When you watch a movie or television show where the character playing a police officer is scripted to plant evidence to frame a suspect or even a friend as a mean to control or silence them, have you ever taken the time to connect the tonality in which it is written and the precision of the execution? These things do happen. However, alarmingly, sometimes, there is NO justice. The bad guys elected by the people or hired by government agencies get away with it and we need to explore why.

This shifty behavior is also key as to why criminal activities in some zip codes never diminish. Street wars escalate no matter what amount of tax dollars are assigned to counter urban violence. We need to understand it is an industry just like the manufacturer producing baby formula. There are CEOs, managers, investors, and consumers. Crime has its own infrastructure and sadly, sometimes taxpayers are the investors in the operation. We just did not know.

We have seen many crime thrillers where the cop is dirty but is casted as a smooth talker, a formidable ringleader able to maneuver himself into any room. He is the "IT" person ... the Rico Suave of law enforcement. He gets along with everybody, knows all the community suspects, and has unlimited access to the politician's office, both officially and after hours. In addition, he is always on the V.I.P. list for corporate and political parties and let us not omit, having premium hookups at restaurants and high-end shops. He gets to have closed shopping sprees for his wife/and or mistresses. However, he is not a rock star, plays in no arenas, but is a cop or elected official with a lot of *infamous* cover.

There is not much some voters add to change the narrative because they are complicit and reward the behavior with their vote. One could easily chalk up the access to just being a great communicator and people-person. He/she is someone well liked and is there to protect and serve. No, harm no foul. This is if you merely glance at this as the norm, one would have to conclude the officer must have been hired by an elite unit in need of an effective front person versus an individual to uphold the law. This applies to both politicians and police.

The cool, charming Rico Suave character is always a calculated glib schmoozer and represents the reality of someone. These personalities are not merely creatively born on paper; their life of crime is brought to life through the carefully constructed guidance of hired consultants and sometimes the actual perpetrators that did the very crimes being acted out on screen. What better way to ensure the authenticity of the role, than to mirror the lives of those who lived it.

When surveillance is underway, many unsuspecting citizens have no clue that someone at a political level, or even a person with close ties to an officer, has been offered up as a sacrifice to feed the intelligence gathering community to meet quotas levied against them, and they get to stay out of prison. Sometimes it is a spouse with a pack with the FBI or another law agency to turn in folks; in the end, they get to go home to their family.

Just in Philadelphia, there are two main colleagues connected to the Gamble Empire, the former music mogul of Philadelphia International records. His former executives indicted for embezzlement and tax evasion, are awaiting their fate but the CEO, Mr. Kenneth Gamble, of the very nonprofit from which they pillaged, is on record stating he had no knowledge anything criminal ever happened. How does that happen when someone has the oversight to sign government documents and must have financial records certified? How do you not know someone is rerouting money, purchasing illegal goods and services? Informant or Inmate?

You have to ask, is someone here under cover, and if so, what is the intelligence to warrant that recruitment? Who is the real target?

Do we see a cover-up and informant? We will go a little deeper in the next few chapters. But certainly, this is a working model carried out throughout the corporate world when politicians, law enforcement and private citizens are meshed together to achieve the same mission; take as much as you can, hide the evidence, and gear up for the next opportunity.

In the case of the Gamble group, there are so many connected to the fraud, but most are walking the streets enjoying life. I am referencing, clergy, accountants, girlfriends, present-day city council members, wives, former mayors, lobbyists, former and present nonprofit executives, and entry-level workers. How, and WHY?

Now the alarming aspect to this is we do have dirty cops still framing innocent civilians, and the justice system does not always ensure fair representation, especially for Black and Brown people. The sentencing structure is extremely egregious and readily deployed to remove African Americans from access to the voting bloc when charged with a felony. There are many ways African Americans are being squeezed out and shut down, thus eliminating the thrust of their power to function as a powerful voting bloc. Having a felony by US government procedures prohibits one's participation in procurement contracts and grants. Well, it is supposed to, but in the case of the Universal Group led by Gamble in Philadelphia, the placement of the organization's former executive received a nonfederal exoneration; though by law he is clearly unqualified to participate but did. There are too many coincidences here. Who in government would look the other way for a former inmate to oversee millions of taxpayers' funds? The law says, you cannot, but somehow, he did. Who covered him?

Here is one of many news headlines:

Former Universal company's executives indicted on RICO, related charges in wide-ranging fraud and bribery schemes involving city councilman and his spouse.

The other nefarious activities and individuals connected to these criminal rings operate within the notable offices of the "Public Servant." A.k.a. Elected Officials and their cohorts. In the eyes of many poor residents, blindly, they believe these Black and Brown individuals to be the

"Best Hope" for their better tomorrow and support these openly criminal actors with a loyal vote every 2 – 4 years.

Black people, if the "collective" is to rise from the ashes, there must be a push back on complicit positions often taken. Whether you agree or not, Society is forcing you to decide. You can continue as is or take the high road and get rid of the pretenders. Stop voting based on RACE. Just because they look like you, doesn't equate to having a heart or mindset to represent you. Find the best candidate and regardless of race, if the person is the best fit, support based on qualification, not color.

Unequivocally, in some political and law governing agencies, the operations have a cesspool of corruption. Not all, but there is a direct correlation to how information is shared between both law enforcement and politicians; they travel in the same circles, eat at the identical table of secrecy, and share the spoils of the already downtrodden poor disguised as servants of the people.

Between the two factions, one holds the power to turn their corrupt activities into a lifetime of excess and lawmaking. The other lives an equally dual seedy lifestyle; sometimes the law is honored . . . other times the very person sworn to enforce the law, is the same perpetuating lawlessness and tyranny.

Though we are often mesmerized by the performance of some onscreen actors, we should never omit someone did the deeds being portrayed. Some of us have family members ensnared by the circus act. Actors can be the best at what they do, but no one is stellar enough alone to pull off a dirty fictional trick without assistance from someone telling them how it will go. Someone who lived it and scored big in the process.

If there were any dirty slick conmen/women in uniform (some with a badge, the other in a suit) where would the narrative derive? I know we have great creative writers and skilled actors but when the portrayal mirrors everyday life for most men of color as it relates to stings and sentencing, don't you think, we need to ask several serious questions of law enforcement and the politicians that we elect? Where did the accuracy come from? Who covers you from the within?

By the way, a police officer under cover to gather information to entrap a person cannot be both law enforcement and friend. The lines are already drawn, and very seldom are the lines withdrawn.

Those with friends in politics and law enforcement need to ask themselves; to whom are they connected? Not to create a wedge but put yourself in a position of strength.

You never would know if an officer or politician has been comprised or caught by the system, and if the latter is true this is where the coziness increases because they have to find someone to snitch on (to meet quotas); this keeps them or their wife, children, other family members from being targets. They escape having to walk the plank to prison.

You should understand there would be more invitations extended building more trust by sharing some low-level information to disarm any suspicion, but you need to consider, is this real or are you on their radar because of a TARGET LETTER.

Now, we have numerous key figures to explore who faked operating in the interest of the public. Their involvement in contracts, politics, cover-ups, and distressed crime-riddled neighborhoods reads the same: Some are inmates, other's informants.

Chapter 3

Good Intentions Twisted

Sometimes those who begin well, end wrong…Life's twists and turns presents many choices from which one must decide an immediate position and direction without any guarantees. Sometimes the position (stance) and direction is just another connected dot and not the end to the uncertainty. But without debate, all of us have to move forward no matter how dim the light or number of pitfalls in the road. We have to move forward.

In a little southern town in Mississippi called Itta Bena, something special was on the horizon in the early 1920s and 30s (for blacks this was a deeply troubling time as any other) but something was cosmically unfolding. However, what was underway would eventually develop to inspire millions of blacks in America to aim for higher public office, in addition, one born during this period would become a music darling whose latter years would treat him so well cementing placement in the Rock n Roll Hall of Fame. New approaches and organizations were stirring. Though there were white men from the area with great achievements, though unlike the black residents written history was kind to their remembrance and contributions.

Although, most in the United States had never heard of Itta Bena, but the obscure area would become the birth home of two notable Black male personalities. In March 1936, the future first Black mayor of D.C., Marion S. Barry, Jr. would grace the world, and just 10 years prior, the incomparable B.B. King was born here.

Barry was born into a sharecropping family, which meant hard work, discipline, and team effort were ingrained. In addition, the visible disparities between blacks and whites were not foreign to the landscape where he lived. He knew first-hand the effects of marginalization, and how deeply it cut off people of color in education, employment, and certainly in having access to affordable quality housing. One could presume that Marion's exposure to inequality, and certainly racial division, had to build a drive to rise above the limited construct in which he was born. As we follow his engagement in social organizations and academia, one can easily trace the blueprint of someone going somewhere in life and who will do big things. You could see it.

As a teenager, he joined the Eagle Scouts and as a student member of the NAACP he fought for equal rights. This early engagement in civics proved to serve him well later in life.

During this time in America, young blacks did fairly well being connected to strong social organizations with political influence; it was a great training ground to participate in the process of social and economic change and expansion in America. For so many it was the introduction to their destiny in political office.

Marion Barry was an insightful teenager, seeing the ill effects of poverty, racism, lack of access to good schools he determined to escape the harshness of the south that was drowning the hopes and dreams of so many blacks in America.

He was determined to be somebody, and to live a better life. Unlike many of his peers working the fields in the south, over time Barry headed to Memphis, Tennessee.

Marion Barry earned a bachelor's degree in chemistry from LeMoyne College in Memphis, Tennessee (1958) and then began a master's program at Fisk University in Nashville, Tennessee. While at Fisk, Barry participated in the student sit-ins that were spreading across the South. In April 1960, Barry, along with John Lewis, Diane Nash, and James Bevel, traveled to Raleigh, North Carolina to answer the call for organized student protest. He was one of the founding members of the Student Nonviolent Coordinating Committee (SNCC) and was the first national chairman of the student group that would work towards desegregation in the South.

So on paper, he definitely earned a badge to serve in the public square. His early exposure and training made him the man for the hour that would open to him in Washington, D.C. in 1965.

Now before we move the story to the obvious, the downfall, let us address what Marion learned growing up as an Eagle Scout.

> **A Scout is Trustworthy.** A Scout tells the truth. He is honest, and he keeps his promises. People can depend on him.
>
> **A Scout is Loyal.** A Scout is true to his family, friends, Scout leaders, school, and nation.

A Scout is Helpful. A Scout cares about other people. He willingly volunteers to help others without expecting payment or reward.

A Scout is Friendly. A Scout is a friend to all. He is a brother to other Scouts. He offers his friendship to people of all races and nations, and respects them even if their beliefs and customs are different from his own.

A Scout is Courteous. A Scout is polite to everyone regardless of age or position. He knows that using good manners makes it easier for people to get along.

A Scout is Kind. A Scout knows there is strength in being gentle. He treats others, as he wants to be treated. Without good reason, he does not harm or kill any living thing.

A Scout is Obedient. A Scout follows the rules of his family, school, and troop. He obeys the laws of his community and country. If he thinks these rules and laws are unfair, he tries to have them changed in an orderly manner rather than disobeying them.

A Scout is Cheerful. A Scout looks for the bright side of life. He cheerfully does tasks that come his way. He tries to make others happy.

A Scout is Thrifty. A Scout works to pay his own way and to help others. He saves for the future. He protects and conserves natural resources. He carefully uses time and property.

A Scout is Brave. A Scout can face danger although he is afraid. He has the courage to stand for what he thinks is right even if others laugh at him or threaten him.

A Scout is Clean. A Scout keeps his body and mind fit and clean. He chooses the company of those who live by high standards. He helps keep his home and community clean.

A Scout is Reverent. A Scout is reverent toward God. He is faithful in his religious duties. He respects the beliefs of others.

These 12 steps from the Eagle Scout's guide are both empowering and as applied tenets serve as a blueprint to physical wellness, which brings about more questions than we have answers, namely what happened?

No one can contest that little Marion Barry was a leader, his involvement pointed due North, but one would have to query what happened between his years as a young activist in SNCC (Student Nonviolent Coordinating Committee) and being the first national chairman of the student group. It is obvious he developed strategic skill sets that were later utilized in helping to desegregate pockets in the south.

He was driven; a great trait any successful person must have and education was a keen element of this passion. Barry earned a bachelor's degree in chemistry from LeMoyne College in Memphis, Tennessee (1958) and then began a master's program at Fisk University in Nashville, Tennessee. It was reported that while at Fisk, Barry participated in the student sit-ins that were spreading across the South. There were transformational moments in America... nonviolent but a visible demonstration Blacks were demanding equality and change in the public square.

In April 1960, Barry, along with John Lewis, Diane Nash, and James Bevel, traveled to Raleigh, North Carolina to answer the call for organized student protest. In June

1965, Barry relocated to Washington, DC where he began his political career. Armed with passion and a desire for equality for African Americans, he soon became a favorite of Washingtonians. Barry was first elected to the newly minted city council after Home Rule was established in 1974. He went on to serve four terms as Mayor of Washington, DC in 1978, 1982, 1986, and 1994, and was serving as council member for Ward 8 when he passed away. He dealt with several issues that included city administration, public housing, violent crime, unemployment, and DC statehood.

Now just on the surface of reading all the accolades how is it possible that a man this accomplished would find himself caught up in a FBI sting. Certainly, he had the right connections, traveled in the in circles but where did the lines begin to twist and go dark?

As a black politician, he had overwhelming support of voters in Washington, D.C. He implemented many programs and was the darling of Blacks, especially in low-income sectors. A fierce fighter and champion for those who needed access so how does this path get derailed? Why was Marion on the FBI's radar?

There was a joint sting operation between the District of Columbia police and the FBI. As mentioned earlier sometimes the "informant" is someone in your circle: a neighbor, family member. It could be an ex-lover, professional colleague; a friend conflicted with the law and knows all your business. Intelligence gathering is big business in law enforcement and a stealthy tool to eliminate

Black political superheroes from rising and inspiring others. The system will never allow those layers of illegal operations to be disclosed and wipe out their payday. You can do well for your people but do not think of sticking your feet in the big business unions live by. This is how they educate their children, travel the world with both wife and mistress... this is not your game. It is a membership base association and sadly, many who want to play here are the wrong color.

The former beauty model, Ms. Moore was no stranger to Marion. They knew each other for over 10 years with an on-and-off personal relationship but it was Rasheeda, who needed the cover (as an "informant") to keep her walking the streets as a free citizen.

Room 727 of the old Vista International Hotel is where Marion's luck ran out. A jealous scorned woman is the most dangerous formidable opponent a high-power official wants to face. Rasheeda, knew she was not the only woman in Barry's life and certainly not the only woman he smoked crack with and she used it against him.

What does this say about the male ego? Or just the human condition in general?

We know that white male politicians are not squeaky clean but somehow too few of them suffer the fate of black leaders and we need to ask why.

In Barry's case, his spiraling downfall as we know came about partying with the wrong crowd, namely a beautiful sexy "inmate", Rahsheeda Moore who turned informant in exchange for a reduced sentence in an earlier drug conviction.

We cannot gloss over the dereliction of duty and lack of value Barry showed in not thinking for one moment that perhaps this beautiful woman volunteered to get even on a personal note, then cover herself and return to society.

Without question, Barry got sloppy – perhaps bored with helping people and no longer felt satisfaction and needed something else to give that high which was more important.

We have several other Black male officials to highlight, and we will connect the common thread they all shared that led to their downfall, and a gaping hole in political representation for Blacks

Chapter 4

The Lights Dimmed

In 1950, Detroit was dubbed "the most liberal city" in America and unbeknownst to many it was the wealthiest city in America on a per capita income basis and the 5th largest. This once thriving mecca plummeted into economic ruin after the White Flight and those who blamed the race riots for disinvestment of the auto industry. We know greed knows no limits; the relocation to cheaper tax bases and where wages were not driven by union demand destabilized this predominate black mecca.

Though during the downturn Detroit along with at least 10 other US major cities were losing more than just jobs; residents in the poorest communities were losing their dignity, access and lack of legislative representation though their officials were still in office. There were many prominent politicians repeatedly sent to Washington, D.C. to represent the people, but alarmingly thousands of families were still living below the federal poverty level. There was massive funds directed to underwrite public housing but limited and selective federal investment in business creation and expansion where Blacks could participate to create economic power. For decades, it was nonexistent, though Black people continued to vote based on color in spite of the report card their elected officials earned.

However, there was never any shortages in the federal budget for welfare programs that automatically cemented a recipient's ability from participating in ownership. Unwed mothers could not have their children's father in the same home, which meant even if one received some degree of assistance there could not be additional money coming into the family. You were capped at the basic level. Though a better model would have been to allow fathers and if they worked to set a time limited on the public assistance.

This strategic design defunct years of entrepreneurship and demoralized the spirit and ingenuity in so many once thriving black communities when major shifts took place in manufacturing, which was the predominate blue collar work base. Along with coal, steel mills and in some sectors American sweatshops.

We cannot gloss over the impact when legislators do not work in tandem with the business sector to create innovative partnerships. America would not have as many defunct, distressed communities that are patched up if we had more business investments instead of allowing tax dollars to flow into other countries and build their wealth.

Instead of hunters, the landscape in urban cities is filled with imprisoned souls that lost their way and forgot the power lies within, many live caged in high-rises and in sub environments where crime is concentrated at startling rates, and federal dollars are wasted because there is no real strategy to end the mayhem.

Even during President Obama's administration, according to the US Census, Black families living below the poverty rate was 24.4% in 2009, escalating to 25.8% by 2012. Household with females only were worse… over 30% lived below the federal poverty rate. Therefore, the question becomes how you rise from a construct that was built to keep you at the lowest level. Others, specifically, other persuasions, live very well from the plight of poverty. So why would a system do away with the hand that feeds it… educate their children, pay massive pensions and contains the violence because the thugs are relegated to an area, very small living space and little money.

Blacks had many elected officials with long tenure but something ironic dominated their outcomes. Many didn't just lose elections; they went to jail.

To the outside world these men and women were educated, had made some stride but sometimes the ending always read the same the jail doors slammed behind them. Coincidence?

Let us look at **John James Conyers Jr.** (May 16, 1929 – October 27, 2019) was an American politician of the Democratic Party who served as a U.S. Representative for Michigan from 1965 to 2017. The districts he represented always included part of western Detroit. During his final three terms, his district included many of Detroit's western suburbs, as well as a large portion of the Downriver area.

Conyers served more than **fifty year**s in Congress, becoming the sixth-longest serving member of Congress in U.S. history; he was the longest-serving African American member of Congress Conyers was the Dean of the House of Representatives from 2015 to 2017, by virtue of him being the longest-serving member of Congress at the time. By the end of his last term, he was the last remaining member of Congress who had served since the presidency of Lyndon B. Johnson.

Okay, so good so far. A black man, very intelligent, over 50 years of public service so what in the hell could go wrong? Black voters supported Mr. Conyers overwhelming so why would he mess that up? In crime, there is always a partner.

Ethics controversy ----

In April 2006, the FBI and the U.S. Attorney's office sent independent letters to the House Ethics Committee, saying two former aides of Conyers had alleged that Conyers used his staff to work on several local and state campaigns of other politicians – including his wife – for the Detroit City Council. (She won a seat in 2005.) He also forced them to baby-sit and chauffeur his children.

In late December 2006, Conyers "accepted responsibility" for violating House rules. A statement issued December 29, 2006, by the House Ethics Committee chairman Doc Hastings and Ranking Minority Member Howard Berman, said Conyers acknowledged what he characterized as a "lack of clarity" in his communications with staff members regarding their official duties and responsibilities, and accepted responsibility for his actions.

In deciding to drop the matter, Hastings and Berman said:

After reviewing the information gathered during the inquiry, and in light of Representative Conyers's cooperation with the inquiry, we have concluded that this matter should be resolved through the issuance of this public statement and the agreement by Representative Conyers to take a number of additional, significant steps to ensure that his office complies with all rules and standards regarding campaign and personal work by congressional staff.

Former Representative had a stellar start but as we investigated corruption became the creed by which he lived and not the law he sworn to uphold. And his wife, Monica Conyers fell right into the same trapping of access and power.

Bribery conviction of wife:

On June 16, 2009, the United States Attorney's Office said two Synagro Technologies representatives had named Monica Conyers as the recipient of bribes from the company totaling more than $6,000, paid to influence passage of a contract with the City of Detroit. The information was gathered during an FBI investigation into political corruption in the city.

Such a cheap move and another demerit for Black politicians.

She was given a pre-indictment letter and offered a plea bargain deal in the case. On June 26, 2009, she was charged with conspiring to commit bribery. She pleaded guilty. On March 10, 2010, she was sentenced to 37 months in prison, and also received two years of supervised probation. She served slightly more than 27 months at the Alderson Federal Prison Camp. After supervised release, she was fully released from federal custody officially on May 16, 2013.

One could ask was this behavior driven by entitlement or the notion that his constituents would not care.

There were Black Politicians in the early 1876s that never ended the way many of the 20th and 21st century politicians have. There is something deeply rooted, and it is not in the best interest of voters who solely vote on Race.

In next few chapters we will deal with the list … There is a list of notable Black politicians who started with great promise who were broken by the smallest trinkets. Some come from Black political royalty, a few worked hard to land but in the end, they were all comprised by things they could easily afford.

How could a family of great promise lose their way to accept the murkiest of deals, chintzy little things that turned the lights off.

Chapter 5

When The Elite Top 50 Isn't Enough

Most people who make positive contributions to the world do so because of their passion and vision; there is a sense of knowing and understanding of the value of the position being held and awareness to achieve that very purpose. Now what comes with this, though many do not intentionally seek it, is influence and social status are connected, and sometimes folks are not ready to be in that room. Some get to enter very sacred doors where power and intellect, and visionaries gather to strategize about the future, to influence public policy, enrich or diminish education, and redirect commerce. Without question, this realm is influential, and one of the fastest entrances into this mysterious private club of "power" is being elected to office. Though in reality, the membership is comprised of public servants who often shun the very oath taken upon acceptance and what is required to sustain access. A very simple process called "serve the people" but many find it difficult to do when they are in the wrong season in life and driven by sheer *stateliness* and access.

Emotionally underdeveloped individuals will always see the "room" (office and its access) as a playground; though in theory, it isn't intellectually processed as such, but the very actions and investment of energy demonstrates otherwise. The "People's" business becomes optional and not the mainstay, which is one primary reason "novices", should be required to have professional coaches or mentors when given the "people's" power. This encompasses access to even bigger, powerful circles of influence that falls in the lap of persons who are emotionally "babies" and lack experience and insight how to handle and utilize the "gift" of leadership. It might sound far-reaching to some but theoretically, you cannot entrust power to someone who is unproven and selectively turn a blind eye and not be willing to engage in the assessment of how that "power" is utilized. To do so is disastrous and looking at the landscape in most communities of color this is the payout for looking the other way. The future of their children and children's children is already mortgaged and brokered to feed the seedy indulgences of the mighty, the few and privileged because of silly, petty thievery.

Despite being in the spotlight that affords many new possibilities, and having one's work acknowledged and celebrated on the world stage as a major accomplishment, especially if the individual is the first in the family to break barriers of limitation and obscurity, seemingly is not rewarding enough over time. In a perfect world, you would think there would be avoidance of lackluster performances and demonstration of accountability to make a difference for the people who entrusted their loyalty to have elected representation. Instead of an official taking for granted the divine purpose for their existence and contributions owed to the very office being occupied (regardless of race, color, or creed). There is a duty to the privilege to occupy. It's all about service, and when those who deem themselves to be great understand the teaching of Christ about "greatness", we would have more "SERVANTS".

Now, there is much to be admired for the initial hard work that comes with preparing for life, to being equipped to reach further and earn a place in history. It's not for the faint-at-heart. You really have to learn to gamble and bluff when the cards aren't in your favor with hopes of landing well. It's the story that has to be told over and over until it sticks... In the political arena, the magic happens when people catch your vision and back it with votes and contributions; this is where the journey to greater possibilities is matched with unfathomable paradox. Everybody shows up.

In this chapter, we look at the strides of former US Congressman Chaka Fattah from Philadelphia. Chaka, affectionately known, but his birth name Arthur Davenport faded after his mother remarried a social activist, David Fattah, his adoptive father, and the person who increased his inspiration in social matters. However, Chaka's birth father was a military Sargent, not a small accomplishment either to sneeze at considering the social era in America.

Politicians in general, revered as supreme, or in a special class, are deified in the public eye, which induces all sorts of tawdry behavior. The way in which their constituents treat and/or react to them fosters a false reality of being elected because one is above and not because the people need a public servant to work in their behalf. And based on the education and cultural pedigree of the demographic, there is acceptance of riotous living at taxpayers' expense with little to no expectation to demand behavioral changes.

For some, the color of one's skin is enough, and this isn't relegated to blacks; whites have voted for over 100 plus years based on race.

The roles reversed, or at least in the minds of those who serve... power, access, and legislative cover, makes a deadly cocktail for those who lose their moral compass, and lack a respectable "voice" in the circle that brings conviction. When one is morally bankrupt it is just a matter of time, not if but when the collapse is not just seen but felt in varying degrees because of the destructive trail left behind and the lives negatively affected by the transgression.

When the purpose of public roles are reversed and politicians are deified as supreme in cultural settings, especially among women, unchecked admiration is addictive and leads to destruction if not corrected within one's self. Men in power are a tall order that women gravitate towards for access, perks, and other types of favors. Black males in political office were increasingly more deified in the eyes of black women throughout the 50s, 60s, 70s, and 80s. A lot of wasted moments were supported, overlooked and totally not important just as long as their guy was in office. It was almost like a referendum against white folks... We will keep him regardless because he is black.

With the feminist movement waged social and identity warfare against male dominance and other equality issues, women, though mostly white women were gaining strength and increased electability to public office. Black women, some equally as qualified academically trailed distantly.

I think it's safe to say Black male politicians who were elected and reelected consecutively in spite of visible limited measurements or high merits were done so based on race. We have to look at the Black female as a contributing factor of hires and rehires of poorly rated black politicians who meagerly serve their constituents.

In the case of Chaka Fattah, an accomplished individual prior to his run for Congress and was considered a do-gooder. His heart was for access to quality education and business. Early on that is… he did a great service during his tenure in both the state house of Pennsylvania and in D.C.

A snippet of Chaka's record: He is a member of Alpha Phi Alpha fraternity. In 1984, Fattah completed the Program for Senior Executives in State and Local Government at Harvard University's John F. Kennedy School of Government. He earned a Bachelor of Arts in business and economics from the University of Pennsylvania. In May 1986, he received his master's degree in governmental administration from the University of Pennsylvania's Fels Institute of Government.

In his early political life Fattah was the lead Democrat responsible for the funding of the United States Department of Justice and the United States Attorney General. Since

2011, the Congressman was able to negotiate an increase of $30M to investment in DOJ programs that fund groups including the Boys & Girls Clubs of America and Big Brothers Big Sisters of America.

In 2012, Fattah negotiated a partnership between FIRST and Boys & Girls Clubs of America to provide robotics programs to 4 million youth by 2015.

Fattah was the recipient of numerous honors and awards including 10 honorary doctorates and the University of Pennsylvania's Fels Institute of Government Distinguished Alumni Achievement Award. *Time* magazine named Fattah one of the 50 most promising leaders in the country. There are so many other notable contributions made during his tenure, which makes his downfall even more unbelievable.

So, how does one go from the above stellar moments to being convicted on 23 counts of fraud, racketeering, bribery, and related charges?

Are we to believe the "Man" was just trying to keep another black man from thriving and continuing to help people of his hue? Is there a blueprint that guarantees failure though the participants are completely situationally unaware because nothing matters other than being known, being seen, currying favor, and making a few things happen for your inner circle? You know, the process by which a few exceptions are made not to intentionally cause harm but to pay off a few favors. To keep the family happy…

The Bid for Philadelphia Mayor:

In November 2006, he declared his candidacy for Mayor of Philadelphia, where two-term incumbent Mayor John F. Street was barred from reelection by term limits, amid pressure from Democratic voters to keep his Congressional seat to maintain a Philadelphia representative on the powerful Appropriations Committee in the House. His candidacy announcement took place next to the recently completed Microsoft School of the Future in the city's Parkside neighborhood to emphasize his campaign platform of better educational opportunities for city youth.

After emerging as a mayoral candidate, Fattah came under fire from the Philadelphia Fraternal Order of Police for his repeated calls to grant a new trial to Mumia Abu-Jamal, who was convicted of murdering police officer Daniel Faulkner in 1981; he also was criticized for possibly unethical campaign spending, based on new campaign finance rules adopted by the city of Philadelphia. The Fattah campaign defended itself, claiming that it had followed less restrictive federal rules in spending the money, but eventually returned a portion of the excess contributions to the exploratory committee following a settlement with the city's Board of Ethics. Fattah eventually came in fourth in the Democratic primary, close behind fellow Congressman Bob Brady but well behind former city councilman Michael Nutter, who went on to win the fall general election handily.

A look at the federal counts:

In August 2014, Fattah's longtime aide and close confidant Gregory Naylor pled guilty to federal charges in a complex money-laundering scheme used to hide an illegal million-dollar loan that a candidate, unnamed in that indictment, received for his failed mayoral campaign in 2007. The loan was paid back using federal grant money intended for nonprofit organizations affiliated with Fattah.

A subsequent Philadelphia Daily News investigation revealed that nonprofits receiving federal funding and connected to Fattah paid out over $5.8 million to Fattah allies and alleged that many of these payments were ethically dubious.

On July 29, 2015, Fattah and four of his associates, Bonnie Bowser, Karen Nicholas, Herbert Verderman, and Robert Brand were indicted for their alleged roles in a racketeering conspiracy involving several schemes that were intended to further the political and financial interests of the defendants and others by, among other tactics, misappropriating hundreds of thousands of dollars of federal, charitable and campaign funds. The FBI further alleged that Fattah accepted an $18,000 bribe from a man seeking an ambassadorship.

Now, let's examine the deduction monetarily and not mention morally. Then congressman Fattah was paid by the people $174,000 plus benefits, how does a meager $18,000 become appealing? Morally, not only did he lose respect, his wife lost her notable job as a news anchor for NBC and his children will forever be tainted if they decide to run for any public office.

In his national races, Chaka Fattah rated mid high 80s 86-89% approval and support. Why would this not be a milestone worth protecting?

Fattah was very effective as a politician; he was more than merely electable. He knew how to govern. He just lost sight of the "principle" things… serve the people not your ambitions. Many politicians are chosen because they speak well, look the part, blend in with the right circles, but are not strong executives once in office. This was not the case. He knew how to effectively legislate, which makes his spiral downfall hard to accept … But let us look at the psychological pathology:

Has an exaggerated sense of self-importance. Have a sense of entitlement and require constant, excessive admiration. Expect to be recognized as superior even without achievements that warrant it. Exaggerate achievements and talents.

In Fattah's case, I would omit "exaggerated achievements" as he was very effective. Nevertheless, what is highly probable is "self-importance" and entitlement. After all, he took taxpayers' money as a loan to run for mayor in Philadelphia. Any other person would have been swiped off the streets shortly thereafter and definitely not released early from prison.

Chapter 6

The Inevitable

Since there is no such thing as coincidences, one would need to consider the irrevocable law of cause and effect and ask why some things seemingly go off the rails that defy commonsense. Why would a promising rising star or proven figurehead suddenly take a nosedive, ruining their reputation, influence and possibly facing financial insolvency? There is a cause... there is a mission in operation, and normally it shapes out through an enticement to change the influence of power in order to accomplish another mission for the benefit of those connected to the change.

When there is an uptick to gain power or remove someone from power, there is an initiation to peel back every layer; sometimes gingerly, by sending nudges to step aside, but when that doesn't work the warfare escalates to ensure there is no recovery.

Normally there is a national or global interest at stake and the obstacles have to be annihilated so that the business on the table can move forward; even if it's a five-to-ten plan, the players have to be in position in order for the objective to succeed. Occasionally a new buildout is required so it takes a moment to get people in order. For instance, if laws have to be written and passed to further the Cause, sometimes new people have to be put in office. Powerful people look for their go-to person to be the face before the American people in the pretense of working for the good of the country when in actuality it is for the benefit of a selected few.

In the case of implementing effective governance and managing political nuisances, it is the premier gambling tournament of the fittest. No one survives in this sphere without grit, friends in high places and connections to law enforcement. From the FBI, magistrates, police departments, even elected officials. Somebody is watching your back, listening to conversations, overseeing deals. Not necessarily illegal transactions, but various trades be it in the provision of services or the transfer of money.

Decisions are made to monitor the activities of individuals and groups more closely in preparation for a potential shift in power that would directly affect seedy interests. The payroll is huge to keep the flow of information current, and those who stand to lose the most kept abreast of possible windfalls of good fortune or impending collapse. Unequivocally, department heads somewhere know the transactional history in each city and state that are threats to existing power structures and personalities. Sadly, taxpayers compensate the moonlighters that double-dip for the interest of the rich, and those we elect to office.

With this in mind, it should be obvious to those who choose to run afoul of the law because of an elected office and fight against the system that there are monopolies everywhere. No one individual is in charge of anything; there are political wolf packs and dominant forces seated in strategic realms of authority in real-time, deciding what moves to make and on whom. The Controlling Interests are always taking assessments to ascertain the level of influence they will continue to have in the world, and how any negating factors may impede their lifestyle or diminish their power.

So, the befuddlement for me is, when white men go to jail for political malfeasance and honest theft of goods and services, why do black politicians process their fate to be any different for corrupt activities?

What are the reasons the lessons haven't been learned through observation of what entrapment looks like?

Sometimes entrapment is constructed through women to create an integrity issue and hurt their image in the black community, especially if the woman is white. On the other hand, accepting gifts, services, and not reporting the exchange is the other silly involvement most seemingly cannot avoid. What happens in the minds of people with power? The chess game never ends; someone wants you in, and others will stop at nothing to replace you, and voters are somewhere in the middle. This exists on multiple levels; from the White House, Congress, Governorship, State, and with local officials there are POW wows about power, and who is worthy to keep it to rule.

Initially, there is always subtle manifestations, but many not necessarily connect the dots to the influencers behind the scene, but they are malicious forces cutting deals to manipulate freedom of expressions, participation, education, what type of relationships are acceptable and what laws can be written and passed to benefit their empire. If you never considered the adage "no one walks away from power, it has to be taken" perhaps your worldview of public scuffles may look like men or women with big egos just trying to be important and feel entitled. Never forget, it's about the inevitable. POWER!

In Marxist philosophy, the ruling class are the capitalist social class who own the means of production and by extension determine and establish the dominant ideology (**culture, mores, norms, traditions**) of society by way of cultural hegemony.

Systems are in place to control, and even when individuals amass wealth outside of the preexisting order of the ruling establishment, there are measures in place (laws to disrupt) to contain rising influencers. Think of anti-trust laws… the government decides when something is too big, over-powering and restricts participation. Not the individual or individuals who built the industry.

Antitrust laws are **regulations that encourage competition by limiting the market power of any particular firm.** This often involves ensuring that mergers and acquisitions don't overly concentrate market power or form monopolies, as well as breaking up firms that have become monopolies. Examples: AT&T, Microsoft, etc.

This is important because when we finally understand that our participation in society is not just an individual perspective, but also a global exchange, we would look for leaders with the intellect, courage, and conviction to begin addressing what is the sealing off of individual freedom. If you are not connected, you are not in. The primary reason why rich people have political friends; they ingratiate or curry favor to ensure their access is not limited or revoked, which makes them even richer. However, the "access" is connected to the public servants we elect for office and pass laws we pay them to oversee that overwhelmingly marginalize millions.

Having knowledge and understanding of the many systems put in place to control thought processes that governs mobility is imperative to know… such as the **feudal system**, and its impact on society which is the combination of the legal, economic, military, and cultural customs that flourished in Medieval Europe between the 9th and 15th centuries. It was a way of structuring society around relationships that derived from the holding of land in exchange for service or labor. It's the same process today when elected officials exchange our votes for what they need to benefit their family's interests; it's a way to control the influx of money and provide seamless access to the best of everything. And when individualists, activists, or advocates, (there are many names for the constructs) rise up, the central focus and aim becomes how to minimize the influence of rising stars that might shed light on corrupt dealings to bring the entire house down. The easiest way to control is through a smear campaign… Now herein lies the need for the informant.

People whom you may have known for a lifetime are forcibly inducted to work against you, though we also do know many who are spiteful and volunteer to disrupt your life. This too should be considered inevitable because nothing just happens, there are no magic moments where people from your past suddenly reappears and just want to catch up, the tell is the conversations are always about your involvements and present activities sprinkled with a little bit of what's going on in their life.

Politicians are always damaged by those who know too much, that is inevitable.

Chapter 7

When Change Has A New Face

Never underestimate the ardent fight that ensues when advocates, watchdog groups and other candidates that represents the kind of change in politics that disrupts the seamless flow of favors, perks, and cash to incumbents that go unaccounted. When there has been no previous accountability required or demands for transparency when transacting the people's business, any new inquires become a threat. The powers-that-be have their people in place and do not take to change easily. Sometimes individuals with political aspirations and their family members are targets for underground forces that deploy operatives to remove threats that could bring down the entire illegal operations.

An adage says, "Never get ahead of your army"; in order to clean up political corruption, it takes friends in high positions to be onboard and that includes law enforcement. This relationship is linked to having enough informants to report and meet ongoing quotas; they have to have boots on the ground that blend in and knows how to tap information.

Potential candidates who represent a new order of governance and whose names are not on the for-hire list of special interest groups, or individuals that do not show up for small-time set aside deals are intimidating. By virtue, you are target no. #1 if you are electable. The rejection of any advances to make one a part of the secret order of takers is never taken lightly because you have a glimpse into an operation that is not legal and there is a face to match some of the activities.

When the type of political change that could upset old paradigms and create new opportunities through representation the blockers are in full force. We should never forget there is funnel operation: from the White House, Congress, State offices, Local municipalities, with Union Bosses, Ward Leaders, Lobbyists, Clergy (who is one of the stealthiest of "operatives") and you cannot do without the assistance of media networks.

Rules and regulations constantly change to fit the narrative that blocks any possibility of disrupting the existing network of illegal political activity or getting around the blockage setup to contain or marginalize any advancement to infuse new blood in the arena.

There is a forcible demonstration to dismantle any infrastructure a candidate has in place or will put in place to expand his candidacy that favors him positively and put existing operations at risk. We are talking about "systems," a consortium of businesses within the business of politics and all the fringes in jeopardy if seats cannot be retained. The longer an incumbent has served, the more likely there is so much to lose. Now, we are not naive in thinking the next person would not rebuild the same type of base and reinstate questionable activities, but sometimes what constituents get is the lesser of the evil when moral compasses are not aligned to do the right thing and uphold the law.

I can speak of my journey and the process just to get on the ballot during the initial phase of the 2020 pandemic and shutdown. Then the *"stay at home"* order in Pennsylvania like in most states was the cinderblock around the lifeline of my candidacy. Pennsylvania Governor, Tom Wolf, who tittered on not rocking the boat with longtime pundits and other political strongmen, kept ridiculous measures in place that made it unbearable to interact with supporters in my 2020 bid for the 3rd Congressional Seat to meet the signature requirement.

As many attempts my political team and lawyers made to be granted alternative measures to collect signatures to qualify the support, I knew I had, I was thrown every curve ball to keep me from gaining more visible momentum on television, and radio. In addition, since the entire country was required to practice safe distancing, it forced my campaign to downside since public gatherings were restricted to a minimum of 25 – 50 in persons in attendance. This stranglehold eventually led to taking legal action after losing 14 weeks of interaction, which was almost impossible to make up especially during a shutdown. There were no other alternatives other than to secure counsel and file a lawsuit.

Under the governor's pretext of not being an *"essential"* activity the restrictions hampered preparations to expand campaign offices, continue fundraising efforts and garner more visibility. The insurmountable obstacles were by design, the pitfalls guaranteed the status quo would remain in office.

These measures guaranteed incumbents could not and would not be challenged though the very office in question being contested has a candidate who has been in politics since he was 24 years of age, made several bids for city mayor and failed. In addition, initially obtained his congressional seat because the former occupant, a long-standing political strong house, Chaka Fattah was convicted of 23 counts and sent to prison.

However, what we have is more of the same and though the current congressional representative, Dwight Evans is well known from decades of being in public office, his tracks mirror the same marginal processes when he was in the PA State House.

Here is a portion of the oral argument:

Petitioning to qualify candidates and political bodies for Pennsylvania's November 3, 2020, general election ballot is not defined as an "essential" activity under Governor Wolf's March 23 stay at home order or any subsequent amendments thereto. The public health emergency caused by COVID-19 and the various "stay at home" orders issued by Governor Wolf make it unlawful and practically impossible to gather signatures for nomination papers in Pennsylvania. The Governor's website stated, "[l]law enforcement remains focused on achieving voluntary compliance through education, but citations are possible for violators depending on the specific circumstances of an investigation." [1] Further, government officials at virtually every level are directing people to stay at home, to practice "social distancing" and to avoid being within six feet of other people.

As a result of the orders and directives issued in response to the COVID-19 pandemic prohibiting non-essential solicitation Prince Johnakin and his supporters have encountered significant difficulty with and have been unable to have in-person interaction with the senior citizen population of the 3rd Congressional District to secure signatures. Safer and less burdensome alternatives are available. Prince Johnakin has lost the over 14 weeks of in person signature collection time allotted to him under Pennsylvania law.

The news brief goes on to recite *"this suit will allow Attorney van der Veen to demand relief for Prince Johnakin who is a committed, dedicated, and caring would-be public servant."*

There were several negating processes taking place during the 2020 election that directly affected not only collecting signatures for candidates but also the timeliness of issuing mail-in ballots, which in the end was meant to slow down the return of those ballots and eliminate millions of legal votes from being counted.

During the pandemic, many voters were too alarmed to stand in line with complete strangers, it seemed logical to create another system of operation for constituents to have access to express their fundamental right under the Fourteen Amendment.

Voting is a fundamental right protected by the Fourteenth Amendment to the United States Constitution. The Fourteenth Amendment protects the right of qualified citizens to vote in state elections involving federal candidates. Included within the right to vote is the right of qualified voters within a state to cast their ballots and have them counted if they are validly cast..

A copy of the letter to Secretary of the Commonwealth of Pennsylvania from then Postmaster Thomas Marshall.

July 29, 2020

Honorable Kathy Boockvar
Secretary of the Commonwealth of Pennsylvania
302 North Capitol Building Harrisburg, PA 17120-0001

Dear Secretary, Boockvar: Re: Deadlines for Mailing Ballots

With the 2020 General Election rapidly approaching, this letter follows up on my letter dated May 29, 2020, which I sent to election officials throughout the country. That letter highlighted some key aspects of the Postal Service's delivery processes. The purpose of this letter is to focus specifically on the deadlines for requesting and casting ballots by mail.

In particular, we wanted to note that, under our reading of Pennsylvania's election laws, certain deadlines for requesting and casting mail in ballots are incongruous with the Postal service's delivery standards. This mismatch creates a risk that ballots requested near the deadline under state law will not be returned by mail in time to be counted under your laws as we understand them. As I stated in my May 29 letter, the two main classes of mail that are used for ballots are First-Class Mail and USPS Marketing Mail, the latter of which includes the Nonprofit postage rate. Voters must use First-Class Mail (or an expedited level of service) to mail their ballots and ballot requests, while state or local election officials may generally use either First-Class Mail or Marketing Mail to mail blank ballots to voters. While the specific transit times for either class of mall cannot be guaranteed and depend on factors such as a given mail piece's place of origin and destination, most domestic First-Class Mail is delivered 2-5 days after it is received by the Postal Service, and most domestic Marketing Mail is delivered 3-10 days after it is received. To account for these delivery standards and to allow for contingencies (e.g., weather issues or unforeseen events), the Postal Service strongly recommends adhering to the following timeframe when using the mail to transmit ballots to domestic voters: Ballot requests: Where voters will both receive and send a ballot by mail, voters should submit their ballot request early enough so that it is received by their election officials at least 15 days before Election Day at a minimum, and preferably long before that time. Mailing blank ballots to voters: In responding to a ballot request, election officials should consider that the ballot needs to be in the hands of the voter so that he or she has adequate time to complete it and put it back in the mail stream so that it can be processed and delivered by the applicable deadline.

Accordingly, the Postal Service recommends that election officials use First-Class Mail to transmit blank ballots and allow 1 week for delivery to voters. Using Marketing Mail will result in slower delivery times and will increase the risk that voters will not receive their ballots in time to return them by mail.

EXHIBIT "A" C

You can read in its entirety by copying and pasting this link in your browser:

Case 2:20-cv-04055 Document 1-1 Filed 08/19/20 Page 1 of 2

The revision process started from the highest office; orders had to be given to change procedures in hopes potential candidates' supporters would not follow the new directives thus, disqualifying their vote. This was operational politics. Mail-in-Ballot boxes were moved, in some areas completely removed.

What we see here is a system. A system strategically operating to marginalize and eliminate voters from having effective representation. Remember I said earlier when you are not on the for-hire list there are different levels of power aimed to make you disappear.

Chapter 8

Dark Doors

We are told to live optimistically, to always look for the silver-lining and possibilities but very few really understand the deeper levels of operation behind dark doors that lead to dark rooms where evil rules, and plan processes of execution to disrupt, restrict access and make the occupants richer. Many persons casually talk about politicians enriched from serving in public office, but how does one hired by the people able to increase their net worth? Are we to believe public officials are smarter or is there a blueprint they are taught to adhere to that guarantees riches?

I know we often wonder why all the good citizens and leaders of the world don't ban together to systematically take down public figures who are in essence sleazy operatives and a deterrent to sustainable progress. Theoretically it would be ideal to expeditiously throw out the bad actors so that societies can recover from past negating operations and summon the best and brightest of planners, designers, economic powerhouses to construct more effective systems by which society can thrive more effectively. A process and prorated system of operation that diminishes lag time where we could achieve major buildout and see effective measurements quicker by which society benefits.

Without question, this is not a distant thought or formula; the potential, intellect, and skill set we already have NOW. But what we also have that's a haunting paradox and looming in every conversation, a fixture at every meeting and has scared the hell out of the do-gooders is the 3rd rail of operation. Shadow government operatives. They dictate who gets in, who stays out and how to they will stay in power. Sadly, it's through our government looking the other way.

We should know that there's a presence in every room of power that too many are afraid to explore, interrogate or limit its interjection of illicit influence but publicly in campaign speeches will hypocritically tout themselves as reformers and contenders to eradicate public corruption. They show up as a real day "Spartacus" and convinced within themselves they are sent by God to fight for the people. Hmm.

The very spotlight placed on influence peddling many campaigns against, and though laws already exist to regulate, yet politicians continue to be lured into sweet, tangled webs and become bed fellows with this elicit group of influencers. It's amazing how easy they are influenced by tainted deals and connection to a power structure created and designed to subvert by infiltrating government and placing their designated figurehead as conduits to carry out operations. Those wonderful campaign speeches as a reformer suddenly are erased --- the silhouette in the room becomes the dominate voice giving orders even if they never speak directly in the room, their presence is what most fear. Shadow operators connected to dark power with deep pockets are the assassins thousands know to avoid. They take orders from a power structure that's unfathomable to totally grasp, some see allegiance to darkness as a badge and assurance of getting ahead with a partnership that could take them anywhere globally. But remember, we elected them.

Presently, in 2022, in the City of Philadelphia, a sitting councilman, Kenyatta Johnson is a prime example of connecting to these dark forces in the room and influence peddling to enrich himself, his wife and friends. Though when this is talked about among some Blacks, many shrug it off as nothing new. We know White people steal, Latinos, Asians, etc… We know that, but when Blacks cannot keep representatives, they elect out of prison, how will they ever successfully have persons who truly understand what it means to live unfair conditions, be educated in poor school systems, restricted from accessing business capital and create a legacy?

Let's take a look at the charges…

Federal prosecutors in Philadelphia handed down criminal charges on Wednesday against City Councilmember Kenyatta Johnson and his wife, political consultant Dawn Chavous.

The result of a <u>five-year-long probe,</u> the 22-count indictment alleges a tangled quid pro quo involving Johnson, Chavous' consulting firm, and Universal Companies, a prominent nonprofit developer and charter-school operator founded by music producer Kenny Gamble, who was not charged.

Johnson and Chavous each face two charges of fraud that carry maximum sentences of 40 years in prison and

$500,000 fines, among other penalties. Both maintain their innocence and have vowed to fight the federal charges.

At the core of the case, prosecutors allege that Universal offered Chavous more than $66,000 in consulting work in return for her husband's help in preserving the nonprofit's ownership over several valuable pieces of real estate. One of these properties, the historic Royal Theater, was later sold, allegedly to pay off Universal's debts.

Chavous allegedly used the lucrative side work to help pay off her and Johnson's mortgage, loan, and credit card debts, according to court documents unsealed Wednesday. She described the challenge to her "work, ethics, and integrity" as "devastating."

"I'm confident when this is over, the facts will reveal that I have done nothing wrong and my name and my family's name will be cleared so we can put this behind us," Chavous said in a written statement.

In addition to Johnson and Chavous, the indictment also names former Universal CEO Abdur Rahim Islam and Shahied Dawan, the CFO of Universal, as defendants in the case. Both were charged with racketeering, fraud and other counts alleging they "stole" $463,000 in fraudulent bonuses. Both are scheduled to surrender later in the week.

"In essence, this indictment charges that Universal Companies was hijacked by Islam and Dawan and turned into a criminal enterprise," said Jennifer Williams, First Assistant U.S. Attorney.

The indictment ties the defendants to a costly scheme to expand Universal's charter school operations to the city of Milwaukee. Former Milwaukee Public Schools Board President Michael Bonds was <u>convicted</u> last May of taking $18,000 in bribes from Universal execs for work on the expansion.

There has to be a reach to live above the fray of tainted relationships – the free car, insurance, condo used on the weekend, game tickets, dinners and theater events should not be more important than upholding the honor of the office to which the people entrusted them to serve.

So, how did Johnson get here? Here's how operators in the room get politicians to overextend and it is never pretty. As reported in the news here is a brief outline that should be a deterrent, but some see it as a model of operation.

Universal Companies, owned by the famous music mogul Kenny Gamble, of Philadelphia International Records group paid Chavous (Councilman's wife) to influence Johnson (councilman) to use his office to boost the value of the nonprofit's South Philadelphia real estate holdings, which were later sold to pay off debts related to the expansion plan.

Universal posted a $200,000 loss in 2013 related to the Milwaukee charter school plan. That same year, Dawan advised Islam in an email that the nonprofit could sell the asset to cover this shortfall — the former Royal Theater building on South Street.

The organization purchased the historic building for redevelopment in 2000, but it had fallen into disrepair and faced a takeover threat via a conservatorship petition filed by a local developer. This legal mechanism allows interested groups to takeover blighted and disused properties through a court order.

But in 2014, while his wife was retained as a Universal consultant, Johnson introduced a zoning bill in council to alter the parking requirements and height maximums for the property. This new activity had the side effect of forcing the withdrawal of the petition lodged against the long-vacant building.

The nonprofit later sold the decrepit theater for approximately $3.7 million, according to the indictment. Ori Feibush, Johnson's former rival for his Second District seat, bought the building and is redeveloping it into apartments.

The charges also cover another scheme involving Johnson that was allegedly intended to preserve Universal's control of other valuable properties on the 1300 block of Bainbridge Street.

The company had purchased the properties for $3 from the city for a redevelopment plan that never materialized. After nine years of vacancy, the city triggered a reversion clause to clawback the land — but officials now say Chavous and Johnson intervened again on Universal's behalf.

The indictment states that Chavous warned the company about the reversion plan in 2014, the same month the company paid the consultant some $18,000.

> We have to establish that at the end of the day many officials just stop caring ... And when we see these type of outcomes and dereliction of duty there should not be a question or pause as to whether the individual should be recalled, it needs to happen. Not debated but actually done expeditiously and allow the voters to move forward to identify better representation in hopes of getting someone who would do the right thing and bring light back to the room.
>
> Now with this level of corruption tied to a former music mogul turned developer, how is it possible that only former principle employees are indicted awaiting sentencing, a sitting council-member and his wife indicted, but the CEO, namely Kenny Gamble is/was obvious to any illicit financial transactions? I'm just trying to understand

how one can operate a multi-million corporation with hundreds of employees, subcontractors and consultants and certainly there is a fiscal designee (accountant) and you never see or read financial reports? Not ever?

The operation is not small potatoes… Universal Group Companies include several Charter Schools, Housing Developments, Public Housing Management contracts, and the looming dark horse of the property given under the premise it would be developed but never happened, and the CEO never had an inkling of wrongdoing?

Chapter 9

The Lit Match to Democracy

We're at a threshold of the unavoidable; America cannot afford not to recognize the colossal decline and shift in *ethics* and lack of effort to be accountable in leadership. Our society drenched in an *accelerant* of patriotic indoctrination is the tinderbox that is destroying public trust and dissuading civic engagement. The damage to public servanthood is at its worse but matters increasing more now because of societal changes. We are not dealing with the same types of skirmishes that existed during the era of Americana. The present battle is not just to have access to vote, or to be included in the America dream as to why there should be louder cries in the public square, but the erosion of conscience. The passage of erroneous bills that erodes the fabric of the family, allows our public servants to enrich themselves in what would send others to prison is not acceptable. The ongoing conflict to have responsible politicians that are not complicit to subverting the innocence of our children or using their districts to mortgage a higher payday from the highest bidder is outlandish and the tab goes to the next generation with NO guarantee of recovery.

The instability in conscience and lack of commitment to uphold public oaths is the slow burn some cannot see. Though much worse, others see and just don't give a damn. At any cost, groups prop up their favorite personality as long as benefits keep coming even when the spoils are visibly with short shelf life and self-serving.

The plummet to civic decency is our undoing not from sources without, as many loyalists to the collective would have you to think, the unraveling of freedom in America is a methodology to contain and those who once started out with great promise and determination to make society better, are the chief villains and brokers. The meteoric rise of many political officials over time became clouded by bad judgment when they omitted to see the flaws in being a shortsighted chief decision maker and not represent the best interest of the people. The other tethered weights that continues to pull down the great, the brilliant, and savvy fierce-talking politician besides "greed" is arrogance.

We have a political machine of the well informed, the insertion of sappy poetry and false narratives of equality, the appearance of access and unbiased processes that normalized criminal behavior with rewards in lieu of rendering public rebuke. There was a time when politicians were caught behaving badly, they didn't dig in their heels and demand voters to overlook their indiscretion, they went away. The erosion of morality and reverence for God are primary measurements of social decline and when this decline is connected to power, we have an implosion brewing. Every man doing what seems right in his own eyes and answers to no one.

To date, we have had over 323 senators to resign. Some took other offices, though resignations amid scandals were rare: Before Al Franken, who was no. #323 Senator to resign not for taking a bribe or influence peddling, the public rebuke from the "Me Too" movement and their ability to keep the story of his inappropriate behavior toward a female colleague in the public domain through social media was the influential power that made him fold.

Reasons for US Senator Resignations, 1789-present

Executive Branch Appointments: 75

Governor or other state offices: 46

Private pursuit: 40

Federal or state/local judiciary: 37

Diplomatic appointment: 24

Illness: 18

Secession during Civil War: 16

Scandal: 10

Other: 9

Clash with state legislature: 7

Unclear: 41

The states with the most resignations are Massachusetts, Georgia, Virginia, South Carolina and New York. Here are the TOP 3:

GA – 19 resignations

SC – 18 resignations

NY - 17 resignations

According to canvass research by FiveThirtyEight, that canvassed on the other side of the chamber discovered that since March 4, 1901, the first day of the 57th Congress

— 615 members of Congress have resigned or been removed from office.

The organization put in context the reasons why members of Congress give for stepping aside and highlights underlining factors that were taking place in the political era and provided historical context.

The 115th Congress owes its historic turnover to the confluence of two events, one normal and one abnormal. First, there's the start of a new presidential administration. Five of the first six members to resign this session did so to accept jobs during President Trump's administration. That's not unusual. It's similar to the seven members who resigned in 2009 to join the Obama administration and the five members who left in 1993 to join Bill Clinton's.

But in addition, three of the four most recent members to resign from the 115th Congress did so because they were accused of unwanted sexual advances: John Conyers, Trent Franks and Al Franken. (Ruben Kihuen, Blake Farenthold and Pat Meehan announced they will not run for re-election for the same reason. However, a *retirement* from Congress at the end of one's regularly scheduled term is not the same as a mid-session *resignation*, which is what we're looking at here.

The extraordinary string of sexual misconduct allegations brought to light over several months led many people to conclude we are in the midst of an unprecedented cultural moment. In the political world, at least, the data bears that out. There has never been a concentration of sexual misconduct allegations that has caused as much public fallout before: The number of resignations over non-consensual sexual overtures in a span of a few months nearly matched the number in the preceding 116 years (five). And it seems to be a recent phenomenon — the first member to resign for this reason was Bob Packwood in 1995. Admittedly, the organization, FiveThirtyEight stated the data may be skewed; but they were relying partly on news reports for divining members' reasoning, and sexual misconduct wasn't exactly a big topic of media coverage for most of the 20th century. Even so, it shows a public reckoning like never before.

To reflect on the political figures highlighted in this book, we should not underestimate the controlling voices that makes it manageable for these men and women to cheat and steal from taxpayers while enriching themselves.

We have a world system penetrated by power and some with a need to stay in power at any cost, while the world is in a cultural inferno over decision making powers that should be individual rights. However, those opposed to Free Thinkers are led to believe the control of equality and the power to navigate, protect or influence this sphere lies merely in the "casting" of one vote. Therefore, the hunt is always on to identify and support the "Ideal" candidate. The naiveté creates an opening for the power grabbers to exploit weak minds, those who refuse to get information and require performance over personality, which is one of the primary reasons why many communities remain underrepresented and broke politicians become rich.

As complex as politics is, there is a huge gap between those we vote for and the individuals who actually decide what policy issues are engaged; this is why some bills never make it out of committee. The Committee chairs always wait for the "nod", voters don't decide. Most people cannot fathom the enormous influence of a *shadow power* base to direct the flow of information, or the buildout of commerce or lack thereof. Individuals, groups, landmark families that control the output of what takes place in chosen sectors, who moves up, and who is taken down. Some are lobbyists that work within a construct with deep pockets and long-standing relationships. The other torch carriers burning down the public trust are informants with a dual identity and protected by the very lawmakers we elect to eradicate corruption.

In addition, most do not focus on the types of laws passed to fund institutionalized markets, namely child slavery through private prisons. There is never a ballot referendum whereby voters are asked, "should we have private prison contracts for kids" but we do. It should be a barometer to gauge where the real power exists.

The paradox is, though we have limited influence at the ballot box however, when the masses collectively raise their voices, it creates a "pause" in the universe and provides cover for Shadow power brokers to determine what to reconfigure and when to reinstate. This is where our politicians predominately take orders from; we can just call them the "firm." Sadly, those we elect protect what should be eliminated from the infrastructure of operation for monetary reasons.

The lit match in the public square burns consistently though at different intensities because we haven't changed the model or policies; we elect bad actors, replace bad actors, and reopen the floodgates again without adopting better practices or increase demands on behavior. The psychological condition of public officials with unresolved personal issues and unidentified displaced emotions in power are often without accountability. Unfortunately, too many are surrounded by "yes" people; the go-along to get along syndicate that causes even more harm.

Many times, there are silent screams for "help" that are unfathomable and directly linked to self-sabotaging behavior of those in power and is one of the chief cries most often ignored because the afflicted soul looks okay. The troubled soul looks good in his role, says the right things, is seamlessly integrated into circles of influence with other charismatics and people like him, but the devil is always lodged in the details.

In order to lessen the damage to the public trust there has to be consistent civic engagement, and a demand placed on the personal and professional representation by lawmakers. That means we have to dismantle the façade of "patriotic resoluteness" that unifies and is used to rally a power base and grants entrance and participation into government but is heavily influenced by secret societies whereby billions are made.

It is one of the paramount reasons why having the right representation is critical to public trust and the guarantee of furthering progress in society. However, even with the knowledge of having some power to persuade outcomes, sadly many are unable to assess the gravity of our democracy being afire and burning at a concentration of near disintegration not seen since the pull away from the British Empire. Most gloss over the hidden narratives because their lifestyle is still highly functional where their options are not diminished; the vacations are the same, where they dine is unencumbered, and many are still on the "A" List. Nevertheless, the lack of civic engagement breeds an atmosphere where political stakeholders pivot against the interest of their constituents sinuously; they broker deals that are more self-serving than characteristic of the needs in their districts primarily because of the absence of public scrutiny.

When we nose-dive and select not to hold officials accountable because they are our favorite personality, we socially engineer pathways that furthers political corruption and thwarts strategic development in society that redirects progress in local, regional, and national sectors. We have to consider the ill effects of being complicit to block group-voting ideologies; it is egregious, it disregards negative psychosomatic structures of false security with the appearance of inclusion but is absent of effective elected representation.

This is most prevalent in districts where the buildout of commerce is always marginal; what we see in some districts is just enough to show a degree of engagement but nothing colossal enough to transform those they serve. It is another method to keep the financial spigot on.

Sometimes narratives are actually in spirit orders derived in dark rooms to control societal progression. This is when planners, stakeholders and private interest decide on what is to be passed onto public officials to carry out in the interest of shadow power and this is the gateway where many officials are dual operatives: Inmate and Informant.

Once named the wild west of Philadelphia politics there were over 39 politicians investigated with a few actually going to the penitentiary since 2002. Power brokers that won the hearts of the people burned their oath of trust:

Jon Saidel – Democratic city controller. The FBI investigated whether he helped two high-rolling law firms that helped his campaign financially by speaking to two city officials on their behalf in an attempt to get them more business.

Vince Fumo – former State Senator; the FBI investigated him for improperly diverting money from Verizon to an economic-development group. This led to a conviction on 137 counts of corruption in 2009.

Cory Kemp – former Philadelphia city treasurer: The fed went after Kemp for accepting money and favors from lawyer Ronald White in exchange for steering city contracts to White and other White associates. Kemp was eventually convicted and sentenced to 10 years in prison.

The superstars listed below demonstrates the diverse level corruption in government – it is a short list:

John Street – former Mayor of Philadelphia

Rick Mariano – Democratic city council member

George Books – 47th Ward leader

Carol Campbell – 4th Ward leader

Robert J. McGowan, Jr. 61st Ward leader

Rev. Randall E. McCaskill – city deputy managing director

All of the above were charged with failure to properly report uses of street money by a PA grand jury. For clarity, Street money is the cash that funnels down from political candidates to ward leaders to committee members as a process to get out the vote.

I wish the list stopped but we have participants that should have been removed sooner:

Angel Ortiz, Democratic city council member: Investigated by the city for driving in Philadelphia for 25 years, including using a city car for 17 years without having a driver's license.

Robert Feldman, a Philadelphia fundraiser who once worked for Bob Casey, John Street and Ed Rendell: Feldman was charged in 2008 along with the governor of Puerto Rico with federal campaign finance crimes.

Just a few more to demonstrate how minor unaddressed actions often leads to disgrace, conviction, and erosion of public trust.

Seth Williams- the first black D.A. of Philadelphia. Mr. Williams was a city darling to many industry heads: the clergy, victims of catholic sex abuse, community groups, and some of his childhood associates. However, he never received any support from his former boss, Lynn Abraham. In a brief interview, Abraham stated that Seth was the least *capable* person for the head position as to why she could never endorse him as a successor. Ouch!

The feds uncovered over 5 years of bribes taken by Williams where he solicited and accepted a stream of payoffs from two business owners. The kickbacks were unjustifiable, Williams' salary afforded him to pay for the perks, but he selected the "gratis" plan. For instance, Seth took an all-inclusive vacation to Punta Cana worth $6,381 though the city of Philadelphia paid him approximately

122K as DA. Now the next few gifts he gave to himself is a part of the exchange that cost him his law degree and dumb… he took a $3,212 custom sofa, a diner for $502, Louis Vuitton tie worth $205 and several other low budget items.

A federal grand jury issued a 23-count indictment, and later as part of the plea deal, Williams admitted in court to the other 28 charges, which included other bribery charges, extortion, and honest services wire fraud in connection with tens of thousands of dollars. And not to mention Seth Williams defrauding family members and a nursing care facility that took care of his mother. Okay, can we just stop right there: defrauding the care facility taking care of his ill mother.

We know that in every city in the world this is a constant battle, some individuals are not trustworthy enough to handle a certain level of power when those in power to ensure checks-and-balances consistently close their eyes. And for the community with the least representation there needs to be a broader approach to selecting their candidates.

In Philadelphia, PA and surrounding counties within the past 10 years the citizenry witnessed an assembly line of elected officials handcuffed, imprisoned and disrupt the faith of the public. The burning of public trust and lack of conscious engagement created a collage of brokenness not only in the system but unveiled the irreparable brokenness within the souls of people who were allowed to continue on a path of destruction though many new what was happening.

The adage "see something, say something" obviously was discarded perhaps for some out of fear, others unequivocally signed on to the silence campaign for personal benefits and the need to be a part of the in crowd. Moreover, for those who initiated and carried out orders of corruption, this was a blatant lack of integrity that was allowed to operate in plain sight. We are not primarily identifying earth shattering operations, some were as small as just taking a meager $4,000 gift and not listing in the official's report, but these actions were enough to be the spark to set political offices on fire. However, though we identify the criminal participation, the bigger picture or story is the human condition that betrayed the trust of those who put them in office.

Other PA Public Fires:

Ed Pawloski, former Allentown Mayor sentenced to 15 years in prison on corruption charges. A jury convicted him. Prosecutors proved in court that Pawloski made it apparent that anyone seeking to contract business with the city of Allentown had to give to his political campaigns. He was also a former candidate for U.S. Senate. The former mayor sold the city out to the highest bidder and was widely known to embrace the practice of *"pay- to-play."*

    Now, with a calling like this, though Allentown is a small municipality where everybody knows everybody however, when a public official demands *redirection* of contract money (taxpayers' funds) for personal use, where is the outcry. You have to ask how many longstanding family relationships are being protected… There is always a reason NO one comes forward. For the sake of fairness to the hard-working contractors, I give allowance or grace in my assessment regarding their silence. I want to believe the contractors that won awards just wanted to take care of their family without forcibly being integrated into the murkiness of doing business with city government. Nevertheless, we cannot discount the imposed conditions to sign off on the contracts.

Next on the list, though not in order of grievance we have "2012" Reading mayor Vaugh Spencer. The first black mayor of Reading. While in city council, Spencer regarded as a do-gooder, a champion for the little people and well respected by many industry leaders finally ascends to the office of the mayor with overwhelming voter support. Sadly, in short order his arrival to the office of the mayor takes a walk on the dark side when he and his team implements a strategy to hold onto power. With his ascension to mayor, and as the first black mayor in the small city of Reading an outsider could assess the promotion as a cultural milestone. He was known for being a person who cared about people – what happened?

One news outlet noted Prosecutors determined Spencer was running a *pay-for-play* operation out of his office. He was found guilty of nine counts of bribery, one count of wire fraud and one count of conspiracy.

First, we cannot neglect the counts of bribery; this represents many meetings, perhaps lunches, dinners or other types of engagements to bring certain participants together. Once again, the commonality is astonishing. Spencer followed the blueprint or talking points of Pawloski. If you want city contracts in Reading, taxpayers' funds are to be redirected back to my political operation… non-negotiable.

Spencer was also charged for bribing other sitting officials; they were pressed to have anyone connected to their office seeking city contracts to contribute to Spencer's reelection campaign. Here is the gateway used to infiltrate other ruling factions: Spencer initiated his bribery campaign, not merely an attempt but actually succeeded in taxpayers' money redirected to him, which means a few or all seated officials turned, their new role now encompassed "informants."

Added to this *illustrious* list is a town favorite, Rob McCord. The former PA state treasurer journey to jail for the "attempt" to extort campaigns contributions during his unsuccessful 2014 bid for governor.

What we see happen to McCord is akin to the aspirations of former US Congressman Chaka Fattah from Philadelphia when he sought another office. Rob's office entrusted him with billions of dollars and prosecutors indicated he bargained away that "trust" for his personal benefit by also corrupting a watchdog agency to look the other way so he could pursue a bid for the governorship. In former Fattah's case, he used a grant to underwrite his bid for mayoral office of Philadelphia that included other unsavory acts and associations in order to manifest this prize.

With agencies and organizations on the take, this is how we continue to end up with the same narrative: *evil always prevail when good men do nothing.*

Let us venture on to take a look at William Higgins, former Bedford County district attorney. Can you fathom the chief law officer sworn to protect the public would have a conflict of interest between seeking, and prosecuting drug dealers and getting drugs off the street? Why would there be a dilemma?

Higgins was charged with protecting drug dealers from prosecution and offering favorable treatment to women drug dealers in exchange for sex. Stop the presses!

William pleaded guilty to 11 counts of obstructing administration of law or other government functions, two counts of official oppression, three counts of recklessly endangering another person, nine counts of intimidation of witnesses or victims and six counts of hindering apprehension or prosecution. Mr. Higgins definitely had hang ups for power, he used his office to trade sexual favors and he violated his oath to the people of Bedford County – compromising the security of his community and the safety of confidential informants.

Hold up, go back; the D.A. comprised the safety of confidential informants. One can only imagine who these confidential informants are and why they were listed in the charges against a sitting D.A. Perhaps these are other officials charged but released, but now informing the government of operations that run afoul of the law but whatever the circumstance their safety was listed as a primary concern to law enforcement.

There are multiple dissenting groups with shared beliefs that America is definitely for sale; some of these visionaries raised in environments where control and economic power are the only means of measuring whether one has a life of note and worth living.

Let's trek back to Philadelphia County... Vanessa Lowery Brown, Rev. Louis Williams Bishop, stalwarts in the community sadly are connected to the list of those who lost their compass, but were politicians repeatedly elected in spite of their marginal representation.

Call the shots, plan the future, create and dominate the narrative and someone or a few will be the dominate voices in the room with unbridled influence to sway positions. Individuals who control legal procedures, control access to elite circles, the flow of money to wealth builders and cultural enrichment. All of which is controlled by one thing, money.

There is a commercial pun, money cannot buy happiness, and then one actor responds, "You haven't been to Dubai." It is said if it doesn't exist, with money we will create the fantasy and make it reality. Likewise, with power structures in America and throughout the world, laws and ordinances shape a narrative created by individuals with strong ties to the dominate players. It is subtle, though visible yet many overlook the infiltration of persuasive affiliates because of sometimes fake, humble introductions but in reality, their assignment is to gather information, identify threat models to their plan of operation, tie-in to legislative influence and then make decisions to unseat their opponents even if it means burning the house down.

www.ingramcontent.com/pod-product-compliance
Lightning Source LLC
Chambersburg PA
CBHW050705160426
43194CB00010B/2002